Tools

Doctor Tools

By Inez Snyder

ADAMSVILLE-COLLIER HEIGHTS

Children's Press®
A Division of Scholastic Inc.
New York / Toronto / London / Auckland / Sydney
Mexico City / New Delhi / Hong Kong
Danbury, Connecticut

Photo Credits: Cover and all photos by Maura B. McConnell
Contributing Editor: Jennifer Silate
Book Design: Daniel Hosek

Library of Congress Cataloging-in-Publication Data

Snyder, Inez.
Doctor tools / by Inez Snyder.
    p. cm. -- (Tools)
Summary: Michelle explains what happens when she goes to the doctor for
a check-up.
Includes bibliographical references and index.
ISBN 0-516-23975-9 (lib. bdg.)   0-516-24036-6 (pbk.)
1. Children--Medical examinations--Juvenile literature. 2.
Children--Preparation for medical care--Juvenile literature. 3. Medical
instruments and apparatus--Juvenile literature. [1. Medical care.] I.
Title.
RJ50.5 .S68 2002
618.92'0075--dc21

2002006000

Contents

My name is Maya.

Today, I am visiting the doctor.

The doctor will use many tools to make sure I am healthy.

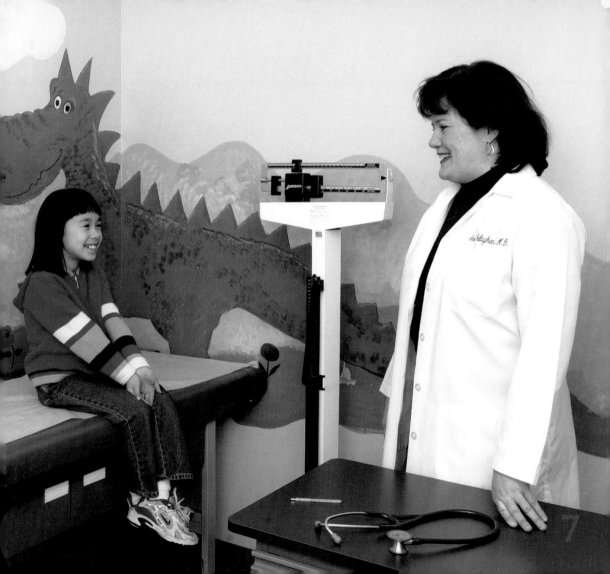

This is a **scale**.

It is used to **measure** how much I **weigh**.

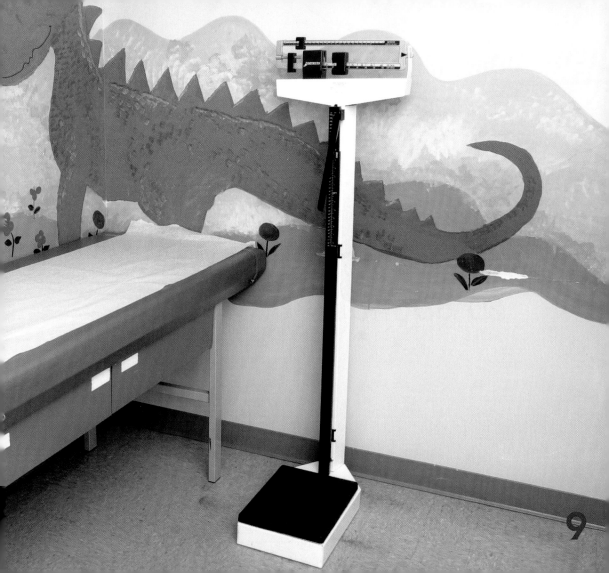

I stand on the scale.

The doctor says I weigh 60 **pounds**.

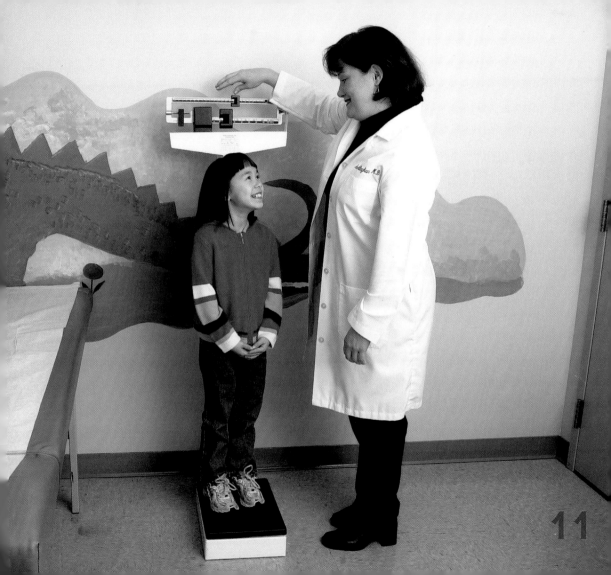

This is a **stethoscope**.

It is used to listen to
my **heart**.

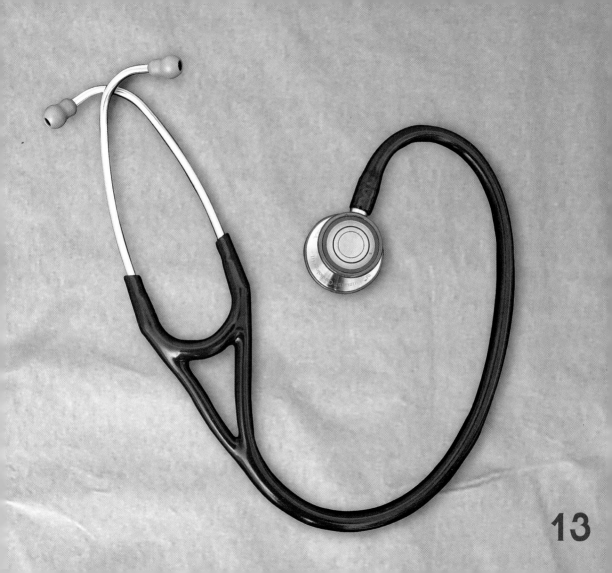

13

The doctor puts the stethoscope on my chest.

She listens to my **heartbeat**.

15

This is a **thermometer**.

It is used to measure
my **temperature**.

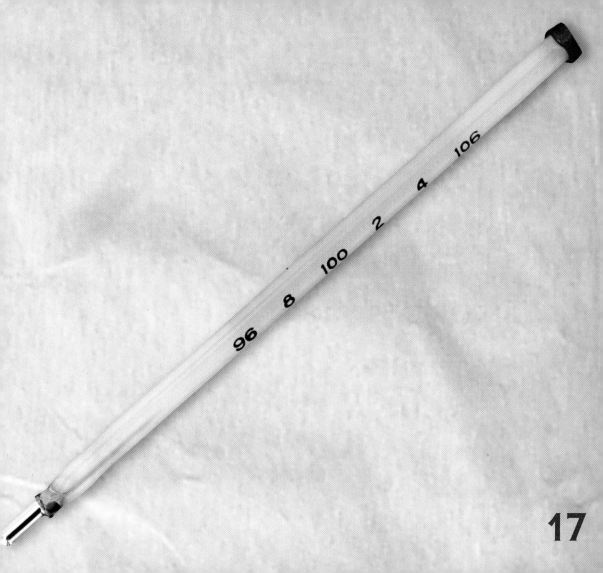

96 8 100 2 4 106

17

The doctor reads
the thermometer.

She says that I am healthy.

The doctor is finished.

She gives me a lollipop.

"See you next time!"

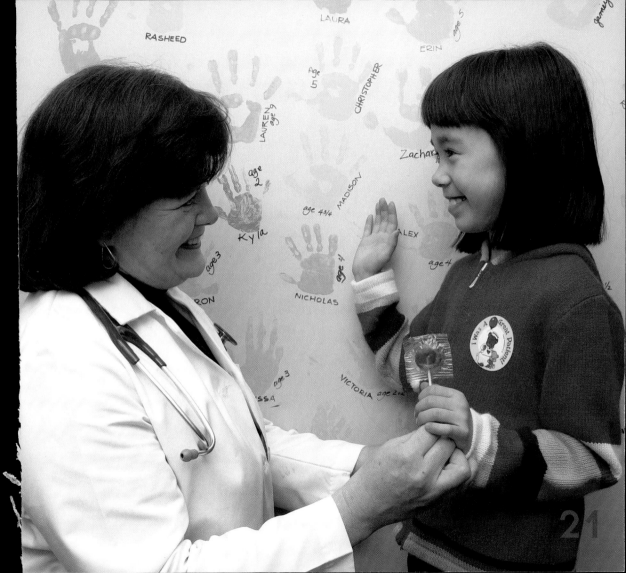

21

New Words

heart (**hart**) the organ in your chest that pumps blood all through your body

heartbeat (**hart**-beet) one complete pumping of the heart

measure (**mezh**-ur) to find out the size, temperature, or weight of something

pounds (**poundz**) units of weight; one pound is equal to sixteen ounces

scale (**skale**) an instrument used for weighing things

stethoscope (**steth**-uh-skope) a medical instrument used to listen to the sounds from a patient's heart, lungs, and other areas of the body

temperature (**tem**-pur-uh-chur) how hot or cold something is

thermometer (thur-**mom**-uh-tur) an instrument used to measure how hot or cold something is

weigh (**way**) to measure how heavy or light someone or something is by using a scale

22

To Find Out More

Books
The Doctor and You
by Diane Swanson
Annick Press

What's in a Doctor's Bag?
by Neil Shulman and Sibley Fleming
Rx Humor

Web Site
BJC Healthcare: Just for Kids
http://www.bjc.org/kids.html
This Web site has lots of fun games and puzzles about the doctor's office that you can play.

Index

About the Author
Inez Snyder writes and edits children's books. She also enjoys painting and cooking for her family.

Reading Consultants
Kris Flynn, Coordinator, Small School District Literacy, The San Diego County Office of Education

Shelly Forys, Certified Reading Recovery Specialist, W.J. Zahnow Elementary School, Waterloo, IL

Sue McAdams, Former President of the North Texas Reading Council of the IRA, and Early Literacy Consultant, Dallas, TX

96